W9-AMA-484

How to Analyze the Works of

ANDY WARHOL

by Michael Fallon

ABDO
Publishing Company

Essential Critiques

How to Analyze the Works of

10

ANDY WARHOL

by Michael Fallon

Content Consultant: Joan Rothfuss, adjunct faculty, College of Visual Arts

Credits

Published by ABDO Publishing Company, 8000 West 78th Street, Edina, Minnesota 55439. Copyright © 2011 by Abdo Consulting Group, Inc. International copyrights reserved in all countries. No part of this book may be reproduced in any form without written permission from the publisher. The Essential Library™ is a trademark and logo of ABDO Publishing Company.

Printed in the United States of America,
North Mankato, Minnesota
062010
092010

Special thanks to Anna Chishom, Contributing Author for chapters 8 and 10.
Editor: Melissa Johnson
Copy Editor: Erika Wittekind
Interior Design and Production: Marie Tupy
Cover Design: Marie Tupy

Library of Congress Cataloging-in-Publication Data
Fallon, Michael, 1966-
  How to analyze the works of Andy Warhol / Michael Fallon.
     p. cm. — (Essential critiques)
  Includes bibliographical references and index.
  ISBN 978-1-61613-534-8
1. Warhol, Andy, 1928-1987—Criticism and interpretation—Juvenile literature.
2. Art appreciation—Juvenile literature. 3. Art criticism—Juvenile literature. I.
Warhol, Andy, 1928-1987. II. Title.
  N6537.W28F35 2010
  700.92—dc22
                                        2010015882

Table of Contents

Chapter

1

Introduction to Critiques

What Is Critical Theory?

What do you usually do when you visit an art museum? You probably enjoy seeing the works of different painters, sculptors, and other artists. You see the many ways the artists have expressed themselves through their creations. Certain works of art might catch your eye and invite you to study them more closely. Yet these are only a few of many possible ways of understanding and appreciating a work of art. What if you are interested in delving more deeply? You might want to learn more about the artist and how his or her personal background is reflected in the artwork. Or you might want to examine what the artwork says about society—how it depicts the roles of women and minorities,

for example. If so, you have entered the realm of critical theory.

Critical theory helps you learn how various works of art, literature, music, theater, film, and other endeavors either support or challenge the way society behaves. Critical theory is the evaluation and interpretation of a work using different philosophies, or schools of thought. Critical theory can be used to understand all types of cultural productions.

There are many different critical theories. If you are analyzing a work of art, each theory asks you to look at the work from a different perspective. Some theories address social issues, while others focus on the artist's life, the technique used to create the artwork, or the time period in which the artwork was created. For example, the critical theory that asks how an artist's life affected the work is called biographical criticism. Other common schools of criticism include historical criticism, feminist criticism, psychological criticism, and New Criticism, which examines a work solely within the context of the work itself.

What Is the Purpose of Critical Theory?

Critical theory can open your mind to new ways of thinking. It can help you evaluate a work of art from a new perspective, directing your attention to issues and messages you may not otherwise recognize in a work.

For example, applying feminist criticism to an artwork may make you aware of female stereotypes perpetuated in the work. Applying a critical theory to a work helps you learn about the person who created it or the society that enjoyed it. You can explore how the artwork is perceived by current cultures.

How Do You Apply Critical Theory?

You conduct a critique when you use a critical theory to examine and question a work. The theory you choose is a lens through which you can view the work, or a springboard for asking questions about the work. Applying a critical theory helps you think critically about the work. You are free to question the work and make an assertion about it. If you choose to examine a work of art using biographical theory, for example, you want to know how the artist's personal background or education inspired or shaped the work. You could explore why the artist was drawn to the subject, theme, or technique of the work of art. For instance, were there events in the artist's past that might have caused him or her to choose a certain topic?

Forming a Thesis

Ask your question and find answers in the work or other related materials. Then you can create a thesis. The thesis is the key point in your critique. It is your argument about the work based on the tenets, or beliefs, of the theory you are using. For example, if you are using biographical theory to ask how the artist's life inspired the work, your thesis

How to Make a Thesis Statement

In a critique, a thesis statement typically appears at the end of the introductory paragraph. It is usually only one sentence long and states the author's main idea.

How to Support a Thesis Statement

A critique should include several arguments. Arguments support a thesis claim. An argument is one or two sentences long and is supported by evidence from the work being discussed.

Organize the arguments into paragraphs. These paragraphs make up the body of the critique.

could be worded as follows: Artist Teng Xiong, raised in refugee camps in southeast Asia, drew upon her experiences to create the painting *No Home for Me*.

Providing Evidence

Once you have formed a thesis, you must provide evidence to support it. Evidence might take the form of examples from the work itself, such as the subject or technique. Articles about the work of art or personal interviews with the artist might also support your ideas. You may wish to address what other critics have written about the work. Quotes from these individuals may help support your claim. If you find any quotes or examples that contradict your thesis, you will need to create an argument against them. For instance: Many critics have asserted that the dark colors in *No Home for Me* convey the depressing reality of living in refugee camps. However, the painting clearly

<u>focuses on tender, positive moments between members of the refugee community.</u>

In This Book

In this book, you will read overviews of famous works of art by artist Andy Warhol, each followed by a critique. Each critique will use one theory and apply it to one work. Critical thinking sections will give you a chance to consider other theses and questions about the work. Did you agree with the author's application of the theory? What other questions are raised by the thesis and its arguments? You can also find out what other critics think about each particular artwork. Then, in the You Critique It section in the final pages of this book, you will have an opportunity to create your own critique.

Look for the Guides

Throughout the chapters that analyze the works, thesis statements have been highlighted. The box next to the thesis helps explain what questions are being raised about the work. Supporting arguments have been underlined. The boxes next to the arguments help explain how these points support the thesis. Look for these guides throughout each critique.

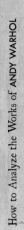

Andy Warhol was known as the king of Pop Art.

2

A Closer Look at Andy Warhol

Andy Warhol was born as Andrew Warhola on August 6, 1928, in Pittsburgh, Pennsylvania. He grew up in a working-class immigrant family. His parents, Andrej and Julia, were born in what is now Slovakia. They were very poor after they came to the United States. Their first child, a girl named Justina, died in Slovakia 15 years before Andy was born. Andy was the youngest of three brothers, all of whom were born in the United States.

As a child, Andy was sickly and often bedridden. He contracted the disease chorea, or St. Vitus' Dance, a nervous system problem, which occasionally caused him to shake uncontrollably.

When in bed, he drew pictures and collected photos of movie stars. Andy's mother bought him a small movie projector when he was eight years old so he could watch films at home. Andy was particularly fond of the glamour of classic Hollywood movies.

In adolescence, he began to suffer from an unknown skin condition that made his face blotchy and made him sensitive to the sun. He became an outcast at school and bonded more deeply with his mother, who also loved drawing and telling stories. Andy's father died in 1942. Believing that Andy was his most talented child, Andrej had saved enough money to send his youngest son to college. Andy showed early artistic talent, so he enrolled at the Carnegie Institute of Technology (now Carnegie Mellon University) in Pittsburgh after high school to study fine art.

Ad Artist

After college, Andy Warhol moved to New York City in 1949. He found work as a magazine and advertising illustrator. In the 1950s, he became known for his ink drawings of ordinary items such as shoes. He became very successful as an advertising artist. He had his first exhibit, which featured commercial art, in 1952. Through the 1950s, Warhol was a well-known and highly paid advertising artist in New York. In 1955, he was hired by a shoe manufacturer to draw weekly ads in the Sunday *New York Times*. The work greatly increased his visibility. In 1957, Warhol won a prestigious award for his advertising work.

Despite this success, Warhol was not satisfied. "I want to be as famous as the Queen of England,"[1] he once said. He always wanted more—more money, more fame, and higher social standing.

In 1960, Warhol moved to a town house with his mother on Lexington Avenue and Eighty-ninth Street in New York. For the first time, he began to create art that was not meant for advertising. He painted large images of his favorite comic-strip characters: Popeye, Dick Tracy, Superman, Mickey Mouse, and others. His other paintings from this time mimicked images from advertisements. Even though Warhol wanted to show his work in galleries, these paintings were shown only in a store window. Disappointed, Warhol kept making new paintings. He was determined to make it as a fine artist.

Warhol learned the process of silk-screening from a friend who was a printmaking artist.

Silk screening often uses stencils or blown-up photographs that are transferred onto silk using a kind of glue. Ink is rolled across the silk, leaving an image on paper or cloth. Silk screening is a very commercial technique commonly used in advertising and packaging. It allows an image to be reproduced many times at any desired size.

Warhol liked the style of silk-screen prints, but he was not sure how much he should pursue the technique. He talked to critics and fellow artists about the look of his prints. They discussed which subject matter he should explore. He continued working through 1960 and 1961 to create a body of work for a fine-art solo exhibition. During this time period, some of his artworks were painted and some were silk screened. Later, he would create the bulk of his work using silk-screen techniques.

Fine Artist

Warhol had determined he would make beautiful art out of everyday consumer products that most people took for granted. Warhol had his first one-man gallery exhibit as a fine artist in 1962 at the Ferus Gallery in Los Angeles, California. In this show, he displayed images of Campbell's Soup cans

and other consumer products. Art critics quickly grouped him with other Pop artists.

Warhol's *200 One-Dollar Bills* was one of the artist's first screen prints.

Pop Art was a new art movement at the time. It originated around 1956 in London and came to the United States around 1960. Warhol is considered to be one of the original artists of the revolutionary movement. Pop artists rejected the ideas of Expressionist painters, who created mostly abstract images to reveal emotions or ideas about truth and art. Pop artists were inspired by everyday objects produced for mass consumption. The subjects of Pop Art were not usually, by themselves, considered beautiful. Pop artists often were attracted to ordinary and sometimes "trashy" consumer goods. Pop artists used images from magazines and newspapers, advertising and consumer products, labels and logos, and comic strips. They also used images of movie stars and other popular figures.

In 1962, New York's Museum of Modern Art hosted a discussion on Pop Art. People at the event attacked artists, including Warhol, who they said were wrong to bring consumerism into art. Critics dismissed Warhol's celebration of commercial culture and the trends toward consumerism in U.S. society at the time. Throughout the 1960s, Warhol remained a controversial figure. However, it became clear over the decade that opinions in the art world had shifted. More and more, people began to understand and appreciate the concerns of Pop artists.

During the 1960s, Warhol became famous for making large paintings with multiple images of Campbell's Soup cans, Coca-Cola bottles, and celebrities such as Marilyn Monroe, Elvis Presley, and Elizabeth Taylor. In 1964, he moved into a large studio in New York that would soon be called The Factory. He hired several assistants to paint backgrounds and do other work for him. Warhol hated working alone. He often let his assistants do much of the work for him while he took credit. A number of artists, writers, musicians, and others came to live and work with Warhol at The Factory. The Factory also became famous for wild parties.

At The Factory, Warhol used silk screens so that he could mass-produce images. Similar to workers in a factory, his team of assistants churned out silk-screen images. The Factory also became a base to make films, prints and paintings, sculptures, and just about anything else that could be sold. In the end, The Factory was many things. It was an art studio, of course, but it was also a social meeting place for all sorts of artists and creative people. It was a showplace for concerts and for other live events. It was a film studio. And, most of all, it was a real factory that produced large quantities of art.

Andy Warhol's Legacy

Warhol quickly became a very successful Pop artist whose work was well regarded by the public and critics alike. Warhol continued to experiment throughout his career. In addition to paintings and silk-screen prints, Warhol made sculptures and experimental films, produced rock 'n' roll records, wrote books, and published magazines. He became a well-known public figure who was a friend to Hollywood celebrities and wealthy art collectors. Later in his career, Warhol became friends with a number of young artists and helped them establish their careers. Many of these artists, such as Jean-Michel Basquiat, Julian Schnabel, David Salle, and Francesco Clemente, became best-selling artists during the 1980s.

Andy Warhol died in 1987 after routine gallbladder surgery. Today, he is still one of the best-known American artists. He is the subject of numerous retrospective exhibitions, books, and feature and documentary films.

After his death, in accordance with Warhol's will, the Andy Warhol Foundation for the Visual Arts was founded. The Foundation has a mission "to foster innovative artistic expression and the creative process."[2] It focuses even today on supporting artists who create experimental art.

Two museums dedicated to Warhol hold much of the work he left behind. The Andy Warhol Museum is located in Pittsburgh, Pennsylvania, where Warhol was born. It is the largest U.S. art

Self Portrait,
1986

museum dedicated to a single artist, holding more
than 12,000 works by Warhol. The other museum
is the Andy Warhol Museum of Modern Art. It
was established in 1991 by Warhol's brother John
Warhola, the Slovak Ministry of Culture, and the
Warhol Foundation in New York. It is located in
the small town of Medzilaborce, Slovakia, near the
birthplace of Warhol's parents.

Chapter

3

An Overview of
32 *Campbell's Soup Cans*

Andy Warhol produced *32 Campbell's Soup Cans* in 1962. For this artwork, he made 32 images on separate canvases. Each image was of a single can of Campbell's soup. Each canvas was 16 x 20 in. (40.6 x 50.8 cm). Warhol painted the images using synthetic polymer paint, tracing the image from a photograph. He used a projector to make the images he traced larger than the source photographs. Through Campbell's Soup can images, Warhol gained a reputation for having a non-painterly style—his images look mechanical and do not show signs of the artist's touch.

The 32 images in Warhol's artwork each represent one variety of Campbell's Soup available at the time. Each is depicted on a white background. Each of the 32 canvasses is very similar to the others. However, they do have minor variations in the lettering of the soup names. Most of the letters are painted in red text, but four varieties have black letters. The sizes of the letters also vary slightly in order to fit the name of the variety. Also, a few varieties use somewhat different styles of lettering. One soup can, for example, uses lowercase script. Warhol stenciled the lettering on some cans and painted it on others.

The Artist's Inspiration

In the early 1960s, Warhol envied the success of three American artists who helped establish Pop Art in the United States: Jasper Johns, Robert Rauschenberg, and Roy Lichtenstein. He decided to model his own fine-art career after theirs. Lichtenstein had selected comic-strip characters as subject matter. His large and precise paintings look like blown-up panels from adventure comics. Warhol's subject matter for his first paintings— comic-strip characters such as Superman—was similar to Lichtenstein's. Warhol abandoned

Essential Critiques

32 Campbell's Soup Cans, 1962

making paintings of comic-strip characters to avoid competing with Lichtenstein.

Warhol looked for other subjects. He liked the idea of painting something he saw every day. He wanted a subject that was very personal but did not look like other Pop Art. An artist friend suggested he make pictures of a consumer product. Warhol chose Campbell's Soup cans. He supposedly ate soup for lunch every day. He made several different kinds of images. Some were very close copies of the original, and some were painted in a more abstract fashion. He then showed these to a few artist friends. They agreed that the realistic images of soup cans were most powerful. Warhol's *32 Campbell's Soup Cans* follows this realistic style.

Showing 32 Soup Cans

All 32 paintings were meant to be shown together as one artwork. Warhol first showed *32 Campbell's Soup Cans* in July 1962, at the Ferus Gallery in Los Angeles, California. This was the first solo exhibition of Warhol's fine art. He had shown work in other exhibitions before this, but they had included only his advertising designs. The paintings were arranged in a single line that

spread across the gallery wall. The viewer had to examine the images one at a time. It was almost as if the images were on a shelf in a grocery store.

Roy Lichtenstein's art was inspired by comic books.

In later exhibitions, the paintings were often displayed in a checkerboard grid, each one blending into the larger pattern.

New Art Movement

During the time Warhol's first show was on display, another gallery close to the Ferus Gallery ridiculed Warhol's art. The gallery displayed dozens of real soup cans and encouraged people to buy three for 60¢. This was a commentary on the commercialism of Warhol's art. It ridiculed the idea that anyone would want to pay for such art. But the resulting controversy about the Campbell's Soup paintings helped make Warhol famous in the art world.

Because the work was nonpainterly and depicted commercial subject matter, many people were at first confused by *32 Campbell's Soup Cans*. The mundane quality of the images was unexpected in the art world of 1962. Paintings of the prevailing art movement, Abstract Expressionism, were thought to be recreations of the artist's unique vision. Expressionist artists held very strict and high ideals about the role of art. In general, they attempted to depict the spiritual and deep emotional

side of human existence through pure color, shape, and expressive gesture. The imagery they created in paint was abstract—it did not try to depict real objects. And the paint was often loosely applied, in wide swipes, drips, or other gestures.

The work of Jackson Pollock is a prime example of Abstract Expressionism.

Art viewers were used to seeing all sorts of drippy, blobby, "messy" paintings. However, many people were not ready to see art that looked like everyday advertisements and consumer products. Many did not feel a traced image could be true art. Initially, many people thought Warhol's technique was a flaw. It took some time for the art public to adjust to the themes Warhol explored in *32 Campbell's Soup Cans*.

Legacy

Warhol continued to make images of Campbell's Soup cans throughout the next several decades. The earliest images, in 1962, were the most realistic. They looked the most similar to advertising images of the cans. In his soup can images from later in the 1960s, Warhol replaced the original red and white with a wide variety of colors such as purple, pink, and green. He began using a technique of silk screening for these new soup cans instead of tracing and painting by hand. Later, he was even more experimental with his colors. Among his experiments, Warhol reversed the image so it looks like a photographic negative or an X-ray image. Today, the most highly valued of Warhol's Campbell's Soup can works are the earliest and most conventional ones. In May 2006, a Warhol soup can image from 1962 called *Small*

Small Torn Campbell's Soup Can (Pepper Pot), 1962

Torn Campbell's Soup Can (Pepper Pot) set the record price for a painting from the series, selling for $11,776,000.

Campbell's Soup Can (Old-fashioned Tomato Rice), 1962

4

How to Apply Reception Theory to 32 *Campbell's Soup Cans*

What Is Reception Theory?

Reception theory is based on the idea that viewers cannot know an artist's intention in creating an artwork. All viewers can know about a piece is what they find when they examine it. Reception theory states that there are as many possible ways to interpret art as there are viewers of art. The ways an individual sees and interprets a work of art just adds to its meaning.

Using reception theory, critics actively examine an artwork to develop their own sense of what it means. They then respond to the artwork based on what they believe it is about. In their critiques, they take care to describe the process they used to develop their ideas about the artwork.

To use reception theory to critique an artwork, you should first examine the work of art carefully.

Think about what associations you make when you see the work. Take your time, and be creative when you try to figure out what the artwork means. Be willing to create your own interpretations about what you see. Then, when you are ready, take care to describe your ideas about the work and how you developed them. Remember that your interpretation of art is as valid as anyone else's, but it is up to you to clearly support your view of the art when you write a critique.

Critiquing *32 Campbell's Soup Cans*

Andy Warhol's *32 Campbell's Soup Cans* is a work of art comprised of 32 red, white, and black advertising-style images of soup cans each on a single, framed, medium-sized canvas. At first glance, the 32 cans of soup are overwhelming in their monotony. A twenty-first century viewer might liken the sameness of the soup cans to the boredom of modern consumer culture, in which factories and mass production make millions of identical goods. As viewers look closer, however, they see many subtle variations in the design and coloring. The tiny variations give the viewer hope that, despite the monotony of mass-produced society, glimpses of originality can still break through.

Since the beginning of mass production and factories with assembly lines, businesses have been able to create their products so that each individual item is identical. Each individual item is interchangeable—a person can buy any item and expect it to be the same as any other item of the same kind. It does not matter which lamp, which mug, or which jar of pasta sauce a person buys because each item is the same as the others in the store. The items lack variation, and thus lack artistry. The buyer cannot tell which individual factory worker put together the lamp or shaped the clay for the mug. The pasta sauce tastes the same every time.

Surrounded by sameness, the lack of variation and individual creativity can become stifling or oppressive to members of

Thesis Statement

The thesis statement in this critique is: "The tiny variations give the viewer hope that, despite the monotony of mass-produced society, glimpses of originality can still break through." The critique asks what the effect of *32 Campbell's Soup Cans* could be on a viewer. It argues that the works could inspire a viewer to be original and creative.

Argument One

The author begins to build on the point of the previous paragraph, that modern consumer society is monotonous. The author explains the effect of the sameness: "Surrounded by sameness, the lack of variation and individual creativity can become stifling or oppressive to members of modern consumer society."

Warhol used real Campbell's soup cans as models for his artwork.

modern consumer society. Knowing that the items they buy are interchangeable, people may begin to feel as though they are interchangeable, too. If the things a person buys or makes are all the same, what is the point of individuality or creativity?

Initially, the soup can images appear to lack individual variation in the same way real cans of soup on a grocery store shelf would. Except for its label, each can is the same at first glance. Each individual image is relatively large—larger, by many times, than a real can of soup, so the viewer can easily see the images across a gallery. The composition of each canvas, meanwhile, is very simple. The cans fill the majority of the space and are perfectly centered. No parts run off the edge, though the rounded tops and bottoms of the cans are near the tops and bottoms of the canvases. It is difficult to look closer and examine any one of the cans, because they all seem just the same as the others.

At first glance, these cans seem to be another manifestation of mass-produced culture. As replicas of mass produced items, they may produce the same response in the viewer. <u>A viewer who feels that mass-produced modern life stops individuality and creativity might interpret</u>

> **Argument Two**
> This paragraph presents several small points first to build to the argument in its final sentence: "A viewer who feels that mass-produced modern life stops individuality and creativity might interpret *32 Campbell's Soup Cans* as another example of cookie-cutter items that do not allow for individual difference." In the rest of the critique, the author will argue that this reaction to the artwork is incomplete.

32 Campbell's Soup Cans as another example of cookie-cutter items that do not allow for individual difference.

However, when viewers do look more closely, they see the soup cans have more differences than appear at first glance. For instance, the size and color of the letters on the labels vary from can to can. Most of the soup names are painted in red block capital letters. Four varieties, however, have black lettering. One variety, "CLAM CHOWDER," has extra black lettering that reads "MANHATTAN STYLE." Other varieties of soup also have extra black, or sometimes red, lettering. In a few of the cans, the font is different. While most soup varieties are written in block capital letters, "Old-fashioned Tomato Rice" is written with some lowercase letters. There are certain flaws, including sloppy edges and broken lines, that mar the perfection of the images.

The effect of these variations is to show the viewer that individual difference and creativity are still possible in a mass-produced world. It is almost as if an anonymous

Argument Three

Finally, the author presents the main argument of the critique, what the actual effect of the artworks is: "The effect of these variations is to show the viewer that individual difference and creativity are still possible in a mass-produced world."

factory worker started autographing lamps, or one cook started seasoning the pasta sauce a little differently. The *32 Campbell's Soup Cans* are not coldly identical—the viewer can tell that an individual used creativity to introduce the variations in the images.

The images in *32 Campbell's Soup Cans* were first displayed in a long row, not in a grid.

By examining the *32 Campbell's Soup Cans* carefully, the viewer learns how to subvert the culture of mass production. The soup cans appear to be conforming to their cookie-cutter ideal, while they are actually showing how a person can assert his or her individuality. Even if the world seems to

Conclusion

The final paragraph is the conclusion of the critique. The author restates the thesis and provides the reader with a final thought. Here, the author pushes the argument by claiming that the artwork's originality not only inspires the viewer to be more creative but also subverts, or turns upside down, the same consumer culture in which it seems to be participating.

be overtaken by mass-produced sameness and monotony, creative touches can still break through. In the end, the soup cans inspire viewers to throw small dashes of creativity into daily life.

Thinking Critically about *32 Campbell's Soup Cans*

Now it's your turn to assess the critique.
Consider these questions:

1. The thesis argues that the canvases in *32 Campbell's Soup Cans* are creative works that inspire originality in their viewers. Do you agree? Do you think these images are creative?

2. Were the arguments in the critique supported with evidence from the artwork? What assumptions did the author make in order to make the arguments? Can you find other evidence in the work to support, or to refute, the thesis?

3. Does the conclusion invite you, the reader, to think more about the topic? Do you agree or disagree with the conclusion's argument that Warhol's work subverts modern consumer culture?

Other Approaches

This critique was one possible approach to Warhol's work using reception theory. Remember, however, that reception theory provides analyses of people's individual responses to a work. There are as many possible responses as there are viewers. The following are two alternate approaches. The first reaches the opposite conclusion from the one above. The second focuses on the images' larger impact, not the smaller details.

A Bleaker Look at *32 Campbell's Soup Cans*

Although one viewer saw the imperfections in *32 Campbell's Soup Cans* as a reassurance that creativity was still at work despite consumer culture's monotony, another valid response concludes the exact opposite. In *American Visions*, author Robert Hughes also sees sameness and small variations in Warhol's work. Hughes, however, does not see the variations as creativity. Instead, he sees the variations as errors and as a sign that the artist was not taking the time to clean up his work.

Hughes's thesis is: "What [the errors] suggested was not the humanizing touch of the hand but the pervasiveness of routine error and of entropy."[1] The effect of the artworks on Hughes is not to inspire creativity and hope, but the opposite. Hughes sees a bleak world in which art copies consumer culture, but does not even bother to make a good copy. Routine errors are common, and entropy, or decay, is constant.

The Big Picture

When looking at Warhol's work, critic Michael Fried is less concerned about technique or imperfections. He argues, "[Warhol] can handle paint well but it is not his chief, nor perhaps even a major concern, and he is capable of showing things that are quite badly painted for the sake of the image they embody. And in fact the success of individual paintings . . . has to do with the choice of subject matter."[2]

A thesis based on Fried's point of view could be: The technique used in Warhol's *32 Campbell's Soup Cans* is less important to the impact the artworks have on the viewer than the central images themselves.

Turquoise Marilyn, 1964

5

An Overview of *Turquoise Marilyn* and *16 Jackies*

Turquoise Marilyn

Warhol created *Turquoise Marilyn* in 1964. It is a silk-screen image of the glamorous actress Marilyn Monroe on a bright turquoise background. In it, Warhol focuses very closely on the subject's face and head. In fact, no other part of Marilyn Monroe's body, not her shoulder or arms or chest, appears in the image. The subject's bright gold hair, her ruby red lips, and her pink face are set off by the turquoise background. The coloring is also balanced. A shade very similar to the turquoise background comprises Marilyn's eye shadow. It is also in her eyes.

Warhol created the image using a publicity photograph of the actress. *Turquoise Marilyn* was one of many images of the actress created by Warhol. The total size of *Turquoise Marilyn* is 40 x 40 in. (1.01 x 1.01 m).

Warhol's Inspiration

Ever since he was a child, Warhol had been fascinated with movie stars and other pop culture figures. In August 1962, Warhol was working on silk-screen prints of the actors Troy Donahue and Warren Beatty. Then, on August 5, Marilyn Monroe was found dead in her home in Los Angeles, California. Authorities believe she probably died from an overdose of a type of sleeping pill. Marilyn was 36 years old.

The day after Marilyn died, Warhol made a silk-screen image of her face. Warhol used an iconic photograph of the actress taken from the film *Niagara*. He painted the canvas certain colors in acrylic paint, and then he silk-screen printed the image of Marilyn's face over the colors. Over the next several years, Warhol produced many images of Marilyn in different colors. *Turquoise Marilyn* was one of them. *Turquoise Marilyn* became the most commonly reproduced and referenced of all the Marilyn images.

Marilyn Monroe was a famous movie star and a beauty icon.

The photo Warhol used in *Turquoise Marilyn* was the basis for approximately 50 paintings over five years. In numerous versions of the Marilyn paintings, Warhol tried different sizes and formats. He also experimented with different color combinations. Some Marilyn paintings have yellow or gold backgrounds. Others have bright magenta, orange, red, or blue backgrounds. At first, Warhol painted Marilyn's lips red, her face pink, and her hair yellow. By 1967, his colors became wilder. Marilyn's face would sometimes be painted colors such as blue or silver.

Turquoise Marilyn is one of the most famous of all of Warhol's Marilyn paintings. Financier Steve Cohen bought *Turquoise Marilyn* for a record amount in 2007. He is said to have paid $80 million for the painting.

16 Jackies

Warhol's fascination with photos of stars and celebrities was a recurring theme in his artwork. Besides Marilyn Monroe, another favorite celebrity subject early in Warhol's career was Jacqueline "Jackie" Kennedy, the wife of President John F. Kennedy. In 1964, Warhol produced the silk-screen painting *16 Jackies*. The size of each of the 16 images of Jackie was 20 x 16 in. (50.8 x 40.6 cm). When the entire set of images was placed in rows, the entire work of art was 80 3/8 x 64 3/8 in. (204 x 164 cm) wide. Warhol created the artwork in response to the November 22, 1963, assassination of President Kennedy. Warhol had been deeply affected by the event, which was covered widely in the mass media. Warhol used images of

One Jackie panel from *16 Jackies,* 1964

Jackie Kennedy that appeared in magazines and newspapers around that time.

In *16 Jackies*, there are four images of Jackie, each of which is repeated four times. The 16 images are arranged in a square. Each row shows the same repeated image. In the top row, Jackie is stepping off the plane in Dallas, Texas, on the day of her husband's death. Bright light strikes her face, and she is smiling widely.

The next row down shows Jackie at the swearing-in ceremony for Lyndon B. Johnson, her husband's replacement as president. Like the image in the top row, all that is seen here is her face and head. But this time, she is looking down, and her face shows a mixture of shock and worry over the recent death of her husband. To heighten the effect, Warhol painted these faces a somber shade of blue. The contrast between the top four images and those one row below is jarring; it highlights the tragedy of Jackie's situation.

The next row shows Jackie grieving during the funeral ceremony for her husband. Her face no longer fills the image, and there is a uniformed officer standing behind her right shoulder. Her eyes are cast to the side, wandering away from the scene. Her expression is blank, as if she has absorbed the pain and shock of her husband's death and has gone numb. Warhol allows her more privacy in this moment, drawing back and not focusing on her face quite as much as in the top two rows.

Finally, the bottom row shows a happier version of Jackie. She is riding in a limousine immediately before the assassination. Again, she is smiling.

Jackie became a fashion icon when her husband became president in 1961.

Although the images in this row are also tinted blue, the color is a warmer shade than in row two.

There are several versions of *16 Jackies*. They vary only slightly, mostly in how the images are colored. Warhol created the *16 Jackies* shortly after the Marilyn Monroe images. Critics at the time concluded that Warhol had become fascinated with dark subjects, such as death and tragedy. Other paintings he made at the time include images of accidents and electric chairs.

16 Jackies, 1964

Chapter

6

How to Apply Biographical Criticism to *Turquoise Marilyn* and *16 Jackies*

What Is Biographical Criticism?

Biographical criticism is a method for critiquing art that takes into account details from the artist's life. Many artists have had life experiences that are colorful, challenging, or troubled. Some artists struggle with drug addiction, for example. Others grew up in poverty or faced other difficulties. Some artists channel happy or exciting experiences into their art. Critics using biographical criticism believe an artist's life experiences influence what he or she paints.

To critique art using biographical criticism, begin by researching the artist's life. Look for major life patterns or important events that may have influenced the artist's outlook on life. This information can give clues about the meaning of the artist's work. However, remember that biography

Warhol replicated the same image of Marilyn Monroe many times in different colors.

is not a perfect map for understanding art. Making a work of art is not the same as telling one's life story. Life experiences usually have only an indirect influence on what an artist paints or sculpts. With a bit of detective work, however, you may find important connections between a work of art and the life of the artist who made it.

Critiquing *Turquoise Marilyn* and *16 Jackies*

Warhol began his career exploring imagery that fascinated and repelled him. As a sickly and isolated child, he was drawn to Hollywood promotional photos of stars and starlets. He also had a fear of death and disease, both from his own struggles with illness and from the death of his father. Warhol's own fascination with beautiful and tragic women, as shown in *16 Jackies* and *Turquoise Marilyn*, came out of the traumas of the artist's childhood.

Warhol, by his own confessions, was a complicated and conflicted person. At times, he claimed he could not bear to be alone. And at other times he essentially claimed he was a loner. In an autobiographical book, he wrote in one chapter that he had no psychological problems. Then, in another chapter, he claimed he had three nervous breakdowns when he was a child. He also admitted how jealous he could be. "I get jealousy attacks all the time," he wrote. "I may be one of the most jealous people in the world. . . .

> **Thesis Statement**
> The thesis in this critique is: "Warhol's own fascination with beautiful and tragic women, as shown in *16 Jackies* and *Turquoise Marilyn*, came out of the traumas of the artist's childhood." This thesis addresses the question: Why was Warhol fascinated with beautiful and tragic women?

> **Argument One**
> The author's first point in the critique is: "Warhol, by his own confessions, was a complicated and conflicted person." This sets up an important detail about the artist that the author will build upon later in the critique.

Basically, I go crazy when I can't have first choice on absolutely everything. . . . As a matter of fact, I'm always trying to buy things and people just because I'm so jealous somebody else might buy them."[1]

Warhol's complicated and conflicted psychology may have been a result of his difficult childhood. In third grade, Warhol developed a disease called chorea. This affliction of the nervous system causes involuntary movements of the arms and legs. He soon began to suffer from an unrelated skin condition that caused his face to look blotchy. In part because of these difficulties, he became an outcast at school. Often, when he suffered an attack of nerves, he was confined to his bed for long periods of time. During his spells of illness, Warhol bonded strongly with his mother. He spent a lot of time with her as a child, accompanying her on shopping trips.

Warhol's worship of the glamour and beauty of figures such as Marilyn Monroe and Jackie Kennedy goes back to his childhood. <u>Unable to connect with his peers, and often ill and alone, Warhol escaped in Hollywood fantasies.</u> He listened to radio shows and collected pictures of movie stars. He also kept a scrapbook of photos of Hollywood stars and other icons. He was particularly fond of child actor Shirley Temple. He wrote

Much biographical criticism about Warhol has centered on his fascination with beautiful women.

> **Argument Three**
> This paragraph explains what Warhol did to cope with his trouble: "Unable to connect with his peers, and often ill and alone, Warhol escaped in Hollywood fantasies."
> This argument begins to link Warhol's traumatic childhood to glamorous women.

to her requesting an autographed photo, and he dreamed of becoming a tap dancer like her. Warhol even once said that when he was young, he turned to movies to learn what love was all about.

When Warhol was 13, he suffered another traumatic event. His father, who had suffered from several health problems, died in May 1942. In keeping with the customs of the family's church, Warhol's father's dead body was laid out for three days in the downstairs of his parents' house. Warhol was terrified of seeing a dead person. He hid under his bed and refused to look at his father's body. The trauma of death and tragedy would continue to fascinate and repel the artist throughout his career.

The images of Marilyn Monroe and Jackie Kennedy couple Warhol's obsession with glamour with his fear of death. They both depict glamorous and famous women who are associated with sudden death.

Warhol made his first silk-screen image of Marilyn Monroe the day after she died from a drug overdose. And his first images of Jackie

---

Argument Four

This paragraph shows how the major themes of the critique come together in Warhol's *16 Jackies* and *Turquoise Marilyn*: "The images of Marilyn Monroe and Jackie Kennedy couple Warhol's obsession with glamour with his fear of death."

Kennedy followed the assassination of her husband, President John F. Kennedy.

As a young boy, Warhol admired child actor Shirley Temple.

Warhol made images of both Marilyn Monroe and Jackie Kennedy for several years. Warhol's life

Conclusion

This is the critique's conclusion. It gives the reader a final thought to consider. It asserts that Warhol's personal connection to the works make them compelling.

experiences made these particular women important to the artist because their stories combined his love of glamour with his fear of death. Warhol was able to turn his respect and worship of these beautiful, tragic women into compelling and meaningful art. Today, Warhol's depictions of Marilyn Monroe and Jackie Kennedy remain among his most highly prized works.

Thinking Critically about *Turquoise Marilyn* and *16 Jackies*

Now it's your turn to assess the critique. Consider the following questions:

1. The thesis asserts that Warhol was moved to create images of beautiful and tragic women because of events from his childhood. Do you think the thesis is convincing? What are other reasons Warhol might have chosen such images?

2. Do you think the arguments in the critique are well supported by evidence? What is the strongest argument in the critique? What is the weakest?

3. The conclusion asserts that Warhol's personal connection to his images makes the works of art compelling. Do you think these works of art are interesting? Do you feel differently about them now that you know more about the artist's life?

Other Approaches

The previous critique is only one of many ways to apply biographical criticism to *16 Jackies* and *Turquoise Marilyn*. Remember that although an artist's biography is always present in the background, artists do not always consciously create images directly from their life stories. The following critics have used other aspects of Warhol's life to critique his work. The first speculates on the artist's use of technique. The second considers the artist's work in light of his sexuality.

Warhol as Machine

Warhol once told an interviewer, "I want to be a machine."[2] Many critics interested in biography have examined this quote. One way to apply this quote to Warhol's works is to examine technique. The thesis to a biographical critique based on this quote could be: Warhol used screen printing, a mechanical technique, in order to become more like a machine.

The Artist's Sexuality

Warhol was homosexual, and he moved in New York social circles with many other famous homosexual artists and writers. Some critics who study art in the context of its creator's sexuality study Warhol's work through this lens. Other critics argue that Warhol's "work is not primarily to represent gay relations" and should be considered on other terms.[3] The thesis to a biographical criticism based on the artist's sexuality might be: Warhol's fascination with beautiful women, as evidenced by *Turquoise Marilyn* and *16 Jackies*, is a general adoration of glamour, rather than a fantasy based in sexual desire.

One box from *Brillo Boxes*, 1964

Chapter 7

An Overview of *Brillo Boxes*

Andy Warhol's *Brillo Boxes* was
created in 1964 for an exhibition
displaying artwork that resembled
supermarket products. The sculptures
are replicas of real Brillo soap pad
cartons. The fake boxes are made of
plywood that has been nailed together.
The boxes' dimensions are the same
as real Brillo cartons, approximately
17 x 17 x 14 in. (43.1 x 43.1 x 35.6 cm). Warhol
and his assistants painted the wooden boxes with
white acrylic paint to match the white cardboard
of the real cartons. Then, they silk-screened on the
red and blue lettering that appears on real Brillo
boxes. The finished sculptures look almost exactly
like real Brillo soap pad cartons. They are even

closer replicas of consumer products than Warhol's Campbell's Soup can images.

The *Brillo Boxes* initially appeared in Warhol's first sculpture exhibition, The Personality of the Artist. This show took place in 1964 at Eleanor Ward's Stable Gallery in New York. Along with the *Brillo Boxes,* Warhol made similar sculptures of Heinz Tomato Ketchup cases, Kellogg's Corn Flakes boxes, and Mott's Apple Sauce boxes. Warhol's Factory produced dozens and dozens of copies of the same basic Brillo box design. Often, the Brillo box sculptures would be exhibited in large groups of 8, 20, or even 45 boxes. Warhol had them stacked in a pyramid shape or in rows along the floor. When the boxes first appeared in a gallery exhibition, Warhol filled the space with so many boxes it looked like a "grocery warehouse."[1] With *Brillo Boxes*, Warhol was referencing an assembly-line method of creating art. He was attempting to recreate the sense of the original consumer product in his sculptures.

The Artist's Inspiration

Warhol's interest in making *Brillo Boxes* was a logical extension of his fascination with consumer

Property fro
THE HELGA AND V
LAUFFS COLLE

products. Warhol was becoming more and more interested in blurring the line between mass-produced consumer objects and handmade art. He wanted to change the conventions of art and the way people perceived what an artist did. Warhol thought

Warhol created other packages similar to his *Brillo Boxes.*

it was suitable for an artist to create "products." The very fact that the artist brought his ideas to the work of art was enough to make it art.

Reception

As with Warhol's Campbell's Soup can images, many viewers were confused by the new boxes. They did not understand why the sculptures were so similar to the real object. Many critics felt Warhol should be creating his own images, rather than replicating commercial products.

Some critics, on the other hand, found *Brillo Boxes* to be revolutionary. The critic Arthur Danto, for instance, thought Warhol's *Brillo Boxes* changed art forever. He believed it had become possible for nearly anything to be considered art. As a philosopher, Danto asked questions about the relationship between common objects and art objects. Danto found this issue so compelling and complicated, and *Brillo Boxes* so important, that he was inspired to write his first book on art, *The Transformation of the Commonplace*.

As he had done before in his art career, Warhol used his Brillo box sculptures to force his viewers to expand their idea of what art could be. Viewers

had to accept that art could look very commercial and superficial. This led to an overall widening of the definition of art.

Warhol's *Brillo Boxes* is usually exhibited in large stacks.

The artist in front of his *Brillo Boxes*

8

How to Apply Marxist Theory to *Brillo Boxes*

What Is Marxist Theory?

Marxist criticism is derived from the political philosophy of Marxism. Marxists believe human history develops and changes based on people's relationships to material necessities. Marxism is drawn from the theories of nineteenth-century German philosophers Karl Marx (1818–1883) and Friedrich Engels (1820–1895). Essentially, Marxism is a critique of capitalism.

Marx and Engels believed that people's relationships to their material surroundings determine their activities, including politics, the law, religion, art, and literature. According to Marx, in a capitalist society, one small group of people, the dominant and wealthy class, hold extreme power over others. They control or own the means of production—the machines, factories, and labor

Row after row of Campbell's Soup boxes fill the floor at The Factory. Warhol, *left*, and an associate gather at the back of the room.

necessary to produce goods. Another larger group of people, the working class, actually provides the labor necessary to produce these goods. The wealthy class tries to pay the working class as little as possible in order to maximize its profits. Marx believed the differences between the working class and the wealthy class would eventually lead to conflict.

A Marxist critique of works of art examines
the relationship between material surroundings and
the artwork, including the role of art in society,
particularly a capitalist society. Marxist criticism
is complex, and it often allows more than one
interpretation of a work of art. Marxist analysis asks
several questions, including: How does a work of
art reflect, or critique, the values of the dominant
class? How do works of art reveal the social
conditions in which they were produced?

Critiquing *Brillo Boxes*

Andy Warhol's 1964 sculpture *Brillo Boxes* is
a set of painted and screen-printed wooden boxes
designed to mimic a consumer product, a cardboard
box of Brillo brand soap pads.
Although the sculpture's mimicry
of consumer products might
seem to be celebrating consumer
culture, *Brillo Boxes* is actually
a critique of capitalism. *Brillo
Boxes* explores the line between
art and product, and in doing so,
it shows how capitalism degrades
art into a mere commodity.

> **Thesis Statement**
> The thesis statement of this
> critique is: "*Brillo Boxes*
> explores the line between art
> and product, and in doing
> so, it shows how capitalism
> degrades art into a mere
> commodity." It answers
> the question: How are the
> sculptures in *Brillo Boxes*
> like and unlike ordinary
> commodities?

Warhol's art, *Brillo Boxes*, and boxes of Brillo pads, a product from the store, are very similar in appearance, blurring the line between product and art. Warhol's Brillo boxes have the same dimensions, coloring, and lettering of actual Brillo boxes. *Brillo Boxes* is often displayed as stacks of many individual boxes, emphasizing its similarities to boxes in a warehouse.

Beyond these similarities in appearance, even the process by which Warhol created *Brillo Boxes* mimicked the way in which ordinary commodities are created. Warhol created *Brillo Boxes* with the help of assistants in his studio, which he called The Factory. An actual factory produces thousands and thousands of commodities that all look exactly the same. By naming his studio The Factory, Warhol was likening his artistic process to an actual factory. However, while Warhol's Factory sometimes produced as many as 80 silk-screen prints per day, it could not rival an actual factory that produced thousands of the same products each day. Compared to other artists, though, who could take years to produce one painting or sculpture, Warhol's studio was indeed an art factory.

Warhol's Factory was also similar to a real factory in the way the works of art were assembled. The artists of The Factory were essentially laborers in a factory. They actually made many of the artworks Warhol received both money and critical acclaim for. This was similar to the way in which a factory worker does not receive credit or acclaim for constructing the latest car model; the company owner does. Warhol was like a company owner.

On the surface, *Brillo Boxes* might suggest that all it takes to elevate a consumer good to the status of art is to move the good into a gallery. If viewers look more closely at Warhol's sculpture, however, they can see slight irregularities in the paint and lettering. A viewer can also tell these fake boxes cannot open. In addition, unlike actual Brillo soap pad boxes, Warhol's are completely empty— though, without picking one up, a viewer would not necessarily know this. These subtle differences call attention to the fact that Warhol's *Brillo Boxes* were made by human hands, rather than by machines. With these human touches, *Brillo Boxes* becomes a work of art, not a mere consumer good.

Even as *Brillo Boxes* has attained the status of art, the artwork shows how capitalist culture turns works of art into mere commodities. By attempting to copy consumer goods, Warhol was giving consumers what they appeared to want—mass-produced commodities. Furthermore, by explicitly referencing a consumer good, *Brillo Boxes* points out that works of art are bought and sold by the thousands every day, much like commodities. Because art museums or galleries are in the business of buying and selling works of art, they are no different from any other store that sells products for consumption.

Argument Three

The author introduces several ways in which the artwork and the product are not alike. This builds to the author's next argument: "With these human touches, *Brillo Boxes* becomes a work of art, not a mere consumer good."

Argument Four

Next, the author argues that Warhol's art critiques capitalist culture: "Even as *Brillo Boxes* has attained the status of art, the artwork shows how capitalist culture turns works of art into mere commodities."

By mimicking real Brillo soap pad boxes, it might seem as though the artist is elevating the status of ordinary commodities. However, *Brillo Boxes* actually shows that the reverse is true:

Warhol's *Brillo Boxes* mimics and critiques the way goods are displayed and stored.

Conclusion

The conclusion restates the thesis, that capitalist culture treats art as a consumer commodity. At the same time, it introduces the idea that the artist meant the artwork as a criticism of this treatment, not a celebration or acceptance of it.

Capitalist society treats works of art as ordinary commodities. At the same time, *Brillo Boxes* is a critique of this treatment: It highlights how works of art, which are treated like commodities by capitalist culture, actually hold a very different status and should be treated as special. Warhol's work thus asks several complex questions: What is the role of art in a capitalist society? Can works of art critique capitalism while simultaneously participating in it?

Thinking Critically about *Brillo Boxes*

Now it's your turn to assess the critique. Consider these questions:

1. The thesis asserts that capitalist society treats art as consumer goods. Do you agree with this statement? Why or why not?

2. The critique presents evidence that *Brillo Boxes* elevates consumer goods to the status of art. It also asserts that *Brillo Boxes* shows how capitalist society brings down art to the level of consumer goods. The critique argues in favor of the second conclusion. Are its arguments convincing?

3. The critique concludes that *Brillo Boxes* is a criticism of the way capitalist culture treats art as a consumer good. Do you agree, or do you feel that *Brillo Boxes* celebrates art as a consumer product?

Other Approaches

The previous critique is only one of many that could apply Marxism to Warhol's works. Two alternate approaches are presented below: The first also explores the similarities and differences between art and commodities. The second argues that Warhol's works simply celebrated consumer culture.

What Is Art?

The philosopher Arthur Danto spent a long time exploring how art is defined. He pondered the similarities and the differences between *Brillo Boxes* the artwork and Brillo boxes the product—what makes one art and the other a commodity? He argues, "The Brillo people might . . . make their boxes out of plywood without these becoming artworks, and Warhol might make *his* out of cardboard without their ceasing to be art. So we may . . . ask why the Brillo people cannot manufacture art and why Warhol cannot *but* make artworks."[1] A thesis on the definition of art might be: The essential difference between a work of art and a simple commodity is the intent and the craft of an artist.

Warhol's Background

Some critics take note of Warhol's working-class background. As one scholar observed, "As the only Pop artist to come from a blue-collar background, Warhol did not cast as contemptuous an eye on commercial culture as his compatriots."[2] Indeed, Warhol was widely known for doing whatever possible to maximize the profits from his artwork. One of Warhol's friends once said that Warhol "genuinely admires [common things]."[3] A Marxist critique of *Brillo Boxes* based on this information might have the thesis: Warhol's lack of material wealth as a child led him to celebrate consumer items in works of art, including *Brillo Boxes*.

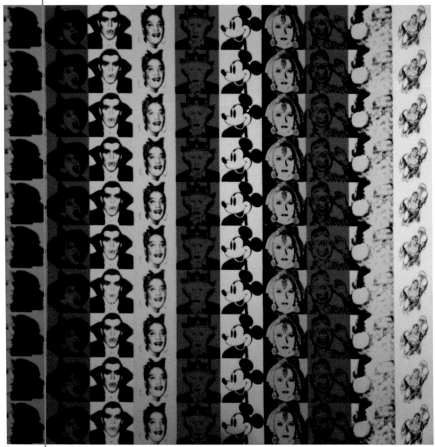

Myths, 1981

An Overview of *Mickey Mouse*

In 1981, near the end of his career,
Andy Warhol created a portfolio
of silk-screen prints called *Myths*.
Warhol was not thinking about ancient
myths. Rather, he was referencing
the characters that defined the United
States during his lifetime. Among the
ten subjects he chose for the series
were such modern icons as Santa Claus, Uncle Sam,
Howdy Doody, Superman, and Mickey Mouse.

Mickey Mouse was one of the subjects from the
Myths series, appearing in several different editions
of prints. In each edition, Mickey Mouse looks
the same. The prints show the Walt Disney icon in
three-quarter profile, with round ears and large eyes
that do not have pupils. The figure's grin reveals his

bright red tongue. But Warhol's treatment of color and other effects is different in each edition.

In many editions, the *Mickey Mouse* prints are 38 x 38 in. (96.5 x 96.5 cm). The character is mostly black and white against a bright background. In some versions, this background is bright red. The comic-strip character pops out in a startling way. In other versions, the background is black. In these, Warhol has added bits of real diamond dust to the black ink, so the character is still emphasized. In this way, Warhol seems to be highlighting the star-like qualities of the famous mouse.

As with many of Warhol's other images of Hollywood icons, Mickey Mouse is presented as a bust. That is, the image shows mostly his head, with a little bit of his shoulders and chest. His large smile and wide-open eyes convey cheerfulness and joy.

Myths Exhibit and Criticism

The *Myths* series of prints were first shown in an exhibit called Andy Warhol's Myths at the Ronald Feldman Fine Arts gallery in New York in the fall of 1981. Most critics viewed the prints as a continuation of the artist's investigation of popular culture and Hollywood icons.

Walt Disney's
Mickey Mouse

The *Myths* series is less studied by critics than Warhol's earlier work. A common perception is that the artist did his best work in the 1960s and was no longer innovative by the 1980s. Warhol's early work exhibits mostly images that were new and current. In *Myths*, however, many of the images came from the 1940s and 1950s, when Warhol was a boy and young man. Some critics see these images as a nostalgic look by Warhol at his youth.

Essential Critiques

Mickey Mouse from the *Myths* series, 1981

How to Apply Formalist Criticism to *Mickey Mouse*

What is Formalist Criticism?

A formal analysis of a work of art is based strictly
on what the artwork looks like, rather than on
its historical or political context. These visual
characteristics include color, line, space, mass,
scale, and composition. Formalist analysis is
interested in the visual effect of a work.

One influential formalist critic was Clement
Greenberg, who wrote during the mid-twentieth
century. He argued that abstract art, specifically
painting, was a powerful tool against the rise
of consumerism and U.S. popular culture as
exemplified by kitsch objects. *Kitsch* is a German
word that describes objects that are in poor taste or
refer to popular culture.

Greenberg defined several key characteristics
of a "good" work of art. First, each artistic

medium should be specific to itself. For example, paintings should be flat and not try to mimic three-dimensional sculpture. Second, works of art should be autonomous, or separate from everyday life. The viewer should not need knowledge outside of the artwork in order to understand the artwork. Third, the subject matter should refer to the artistic process. Paintings should not represent life; they should represent painting itself and the creative process. Generally, this means that art should be nonrepresentational or abstract. Lastly, art should encourage the viewer to contemplate the higher meaning of a work. This meaning should be contained solely within the artwork itself; it should not refer to anything outside the piece.

A Greenbergian formalist critique asks whether a work of art meets the previous criteria. Some questions a Greenbergian critique would ask are: Does the work of art refer to popular culture? Does the work of art refer only to itself? Does it represent people or recognizable objects from daily life?

Critiquing *Mickey Mouse*

In 1981, Andy Warhol created a series of silk-screen prints entitled *Myths*. Although this series of prints is widely recognized and exhibited in museums, according to Greenberg's criteria, it cannot be considered high art. These prints represent images from popular culture. Because these prints refer specifically to popular consumer culture, they are instead low art or kitsch.

Thesis Statement

The thesis statement of this critique is: "Because these prints refer specifically to popular consumer culture, they are instead low art or kitsch." It answers the question: According to Greenberg's criteria, are Warhol's *Mickey Mouse* prints high art?

Argument One

The critique's first argument is: "Warhol's *Mickey Mouse* prints break Greenberg's rule of keeping artistic media separate." The author will support this point with evidence.

Warhol's *Mickey Mouse* prints break Greenberg's rule of keeping artistic media separate. According to this rule, paintings should not mimic sculptures, drawings should not mimic photographs, and so forth. The original images of Mickey Mouse were drawn by Walt Disney using pen and ink and then were animated for the movies. However, Warhol and his assistants at his studio replicated the image of Mickey Mouse using screen printing, a process that involves inking a stenciled image. In some versions of *Mickey Mouse*, Warhol and his assistants even sprinkled real diamond dust on the black background. Warhol's *Mickey Mouse*, therefore, does not keep artistic media separate because it crosses boundaries between the original pen and ink drawings and screen printing. In addition, diamond dust is associated with flashy, popular consumer culture, as opposed to traditional artistic practice.

Mickey Mouse does not conform to Greenberg's criteria because it does not refer or call attention to the artistic practice used to create it, silk-screen printing. According to Greenberg, in a painting, for example, brushstrokes should be visible. A print should look as though it has been printed, not painted. But Warhol's silk-screen print attempts to mimic the original artistic medium, pen and ink. Warhol's *Mickey Mouse* retains the original drawn lines and solid, bold coloring that Walt Disney used to create the character. By doing this, Warhol's images do not refer to the process of printmaking, but rather to drawing and animation.

Mickey Mouse also fails Greenberg's test because it is not an autonomous work of art. In order to appreciate Warhol's image of the Disney icon, the viewer must know Mickey Mouse as a figure in popular culture. A work of high art should

Argument Two

The author presents another argument in support of the thesis: "*Mickey Mouse* does not conform to Greenberg's criteria because it does not refer or call attention to the artistic practice used to create it, silk-screen printing." The evidence in the rest of the paragraph supports this point.

Argument Three

In this paragraph, the author presents another of Greenberg's criteria and explains why Warhol's artwork does not conform: "*Mickey Mouse* also fails Greenberg's test because it is not an autonomous work of art."

Argument Four

The author examines Greenberg's last criteria in this argument: "A good work of art should challenge the viewer to a higher level of thought, which *Mickey Mouse* fails to do."

be separate from everyday life, not dependent on popular culture for its meaning.

A good work of art should challenge the viewer to a higher level of thought, which *Mickey Mouse* fails to do. Because Mickey Mouse is a recognizable figure in popular culture, Warhol's image does not challenge viewers to think beyond their daily existence. The artwork does not ask the viewer to reflect on the meaning of existence. The artwork refers only to the Disney icon. Its meaning is clear and does not require effort on the part of the viewer.

According to Greenberg's criteria, *Mickey Mouse* falls flat as a work of high art. *Mickey Mouse* may be characterized as kitsch rather than as a work of high art. Despite failing Greenberg's criteria, *Mickey Mouse* and Warhol's other works are displayed in art museums and admired for their unique take on pop culture.

Conclusion

The conclusion restates the thesis, that *Mickey Mouse* should be classified as kitsch, not as art. It leaves the reader with a final thought to consider: Even though *Mickey Mouse* fails Greenberg's criteria, it is displayed and studied as art by many people.

Thinking Critically about *Mickey Mouse*

Now it's your turn to assess the critique. Consider these questions:

1. The critique argues that, according to Greenberg's criteria, Warhol's *Mickey Mouse* is not art. What criteria would you choose to define art?

2. The critique assumes that *Mickey Mouse* has no hidden meanings: "Its meaning is clear and does not require effort on the part of the viewer." Do the author's arguments convince you? Do you agree that *Mickey Mouse* has no hidden meanings?

3. The critique concludes that *Mickey Mouse* is kitsch. Are you convinced by the arguments in the critique? Do you agree that *Mickey Mouse* is kitsch? Why or why not?

Other Approaches

The above critique applied Greenberg's criteria to determine that the critic would not have considered Warhol's *Mickey Mouse* art. However, even among other formalist critics, Greenberg's criteria are only one opinion. A lively discussion continues among critics about what qualifies as art and what makes a work of art "good." The first example below presents a formalist argument about representational art. The second example explores the effect of color in Warhol's work.

For Art's Sake

Formalism has been described as "art for art's sake."[1] This means art is done not to represent objects, but to express the artist's feelings or to invite the viewer to think about the meaning of art. Warhol's work represents highly recognizable characters, objects, and people. A formalist thesis might be: Representational work such as Warhol's *Mickey Mouse* does not invite the viewer to think about the meaning of art.

Form and Color

Warhol's work is interesting because he frequently repeats images, changing only the colors. *Mickey Mouse* is a perfect example of this tendency. A formalist might ask what effect Warhol creates when he uses different colors. A formalist thesis about this effect might be: Despite adjustments of color in backgrounds, the true nature of Mickey Mouse remains in his unchanged profile and cheery smile. By subtly changing treatments in different versions of *Mickey Mouse*, Warhol proves that he has captured the essence of Mickey.

You Critique It

Now that you have learned about several different critical theories and how to apply them to art, are you ready to perform a critique of your own? You have read that this type of evaluation can help you look at art from a new perspective and make you pay attention to certain issues you may not have otherwise recognized. So, why not use one of the critical theories profiled in this book to consider a fresh take on your favorite work?

First, choose a theory and the artwork you want to analyze. Remember that the theory is a springboard for asking questions about the work.

Next, write a specific question that relates to the theory you have selected. Then you can form your thesis, which should provide the answer to that question. Your thesis is the most important part of your critique and offers an argument about the work based on the tenets, or beliefs, of the theory you are applying. Recall that the thesis statement typically appears at the very end of the introductory paragraph of your essay. It is usually only one sentence long.

After you have written your thesis, find evidence to back it up. Good places to start are in the work itself or journals or articles that discuss what other people have said about it. Since you are critiquing a work of art, you may also want to read about the artist's life to get a sense of what factors may have affected the creative process. This can be especially useful if working within historical, biographical, or psychological criticism.

Depending on which theory you apply, you can often find evidence in the art's subject, its color and form, or the artist's technique. You should also explore aspects of the work that seem to disprove your thesis and create an argument against them. As you do this, you might want to address what other critics have written about the artwork. Their quotes may help support your claim.

Before you start analyzing a work, think about the different arguments made in this book. Reflect on how evidence supporting the thesis was presented. Did you find that some of the techniques used to back up arguments were more convincing than others? Try these methods as you prove your thesis in your own critique.

When you are finished writing your critique, read it over carefully. Is your thesis statement understandable? Do the supporting arguments flow logically, with the topic of each paragraph clearly stated? Can you add any information that would present your readers with a stronger argument in favor of your thesis? Were you able to use evidence from the artwork as well as quotes from critics to enhance your ideas?

Did you see the work in a new light?

Timeline

1928 Andrew Warhola is born in Pittsburgh, Pennsylvania, on August 6.

1936 Warhol contracts a rare disease called chorea, or St. Vitus' Dance.

1942 Warhol's father, Andrej, dies.

1945 Warhol enrolls at the Carnegie Institute of Technology to study art.

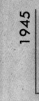

1963 On November 22, President John F. Kennedy is riding in an open car beside his wife, Jacqueline, in Dallas, Texas, when he is assassinated.

1964 Warhol moves to a new studio; it will become known as The Factory.

Brillo Boxes is a part of Warhol's first sculpture show, April 21 through May 9 at Stable Gallery in New York.

Warhol creates *16 Jackies* in response to the president's assassination.

Continuing his series of Marilyn paintings, Warhol creates *Turquoise Marilyn.*

1949 Warhol graduates from the Carnegie Institute and moves to New York to work as a commercial artist.

1952 Warhol has his first exhibit for commercial artwork in New York.

1955 Warhol is hired by a shoe manufacturer to draw ads for the *New York Times*.

1960 Warhol moves into a town house with his mother, Julia, at Lexington Avenue and Eighty-ninth Street in New York.

Warhol begins his first non-commercial artwork.

1962 Warhol begins to experiment with silk-screen prints.

Warhol has his first fine art exhibit at the Ferus Gallery in Los Angeles, July 9 through August 4, showing *32 Campbell's Soup Cans*.

Marilyn Monroe dies on August 5. On August 6, Warhol begins to make Marilyn paintings.

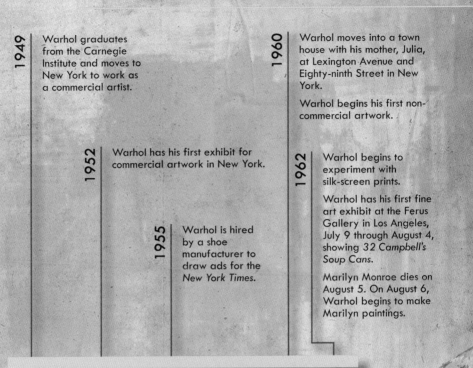

1981 Warhol creates his *Myths* series, including *Mickey Mouse*.

1987 Warhol dies after a gallbladder operation on February 22.

1991 The Andy Warhol Museum of Modern Art opens.

Glossary

abstract
Showing ideas rather than objects.

capitalism
An economic system in which investments, businesses, and the production and distribution of wealth are controlled by private individuals or corporations, as opposed to the government.

commodity
A good that can be bought and sold.

consumerism
The belief that it is necessary for members of society to buy an increasing amount of goods.

expressionism
An artistic movement of the mid-twentieth century, usually abstract, in which artists usually created art to express their emotions or inner being.

formalism
A theory of art that analyzes a work based solely on its appearance.

iconic
Instantly recognizable; famous.

kitsch
Something in poor taste; something that refers to popular culture.

mass consumption
The buying of identical goods on a large scale.

medium
In art, the material used to create a work.

Pop Art
>An art movement begun in the 1960s that used pop culture and consumer goods as its subjects.

representational
>Showing objects rather than abstract ideas.

silk-screening
>A mechanical process used to copy a design.

stencil
>A shape or an image made of wax, plastic, or a similar material with holes that allow ink through to create a design on paper, fabric, or another material.

subverts
>Turns around or corrupts.

Bibliography of Works and Criticism

Important Works

Coca-Cola, 1960 (Oil and crayon on canvas, 6' x 54")

Dick Tracy, 1960 (Casein and crayon on canvas,
48" x 33 7/8")

One-Dollar Bill, 1962 (Synthetic polymer paint and pencil on
canvas, 52" x 6')

200 One-Dollar Bills, 1962 (Silk-screen ink on canvas,
8' 1 1/4" x 6' 2 3/8")

32 Campbell's Soup Cans, 1962 (Synthetic polymer paint on
canvas, 32 works, each 16" x 20")

Silver Disaster, 1963 (Silk-screen ink on synthetic polymer paint
on canvas, 42" x 60")

Little Electric Chair, 1963 (Silk-screen ink on synthetic polymer
paint on canvas, two panels, each 8' 9" x 6' 8 1/4")

Brillo Boxes, 1964 (Silk-screen ink on wood,
17 1/8" x 17 1/8" x 14" each)

Turquoise Marilyn, 1964 (Silk-screen ink on synthetic polymer
paint on canvas, 40" x 40")

16 Jackies, 1964 (Silk-screen ink on synthetic polymer paint on
canvas, 80 3/8" x 64 3/8")

Self portrait, 1967 (Silk-screen ink on synthetic polymer paint on
canvas, 6' x 6')

Flowers, 1967 (Silk-screen ink on synthetic polymer paint on
canvas, 7' x 12')

Mao, 1972 (Silk-screen ink on synthetic polymer paint on canvas,
6' 10" x 61")

Julia Warhola, 1974 (Silk-screen ink on synthetic polymer paint on canvas, 40" x 40")

Hammer and Sickle, 1977 (Silk-screen ink on synthetic polymer paint on canvas, 6' x 7' 2")

Mickey Mouse (Myths series*)*, 1981 (Silk-screen ink on synthetic polymer paint on canvas, some prints include diamond dust, 38" x 38")

Six Self Portraits, 1986 (Silk-screen ink on synthetic polymer paint on canvas, six portraits, each 22 3/4" x 22")

Critical Discussions

Bergin, Paul. "Andy Warhol: The Artist as Machine." *Art Journal* 24.4 (1967): 359–363.

Danto, Arthur C. "Andy Warhol." *Brushes with History: Writing on Art from* The Nation, *1865–2001*. Edited by Peter G. Meyer. New York: Nation Books, 2001.

Madoff, Steven Henry, ed. *Pop Art: A Critical History*. Berkeley, CA: University of California Press, 1997.

Schjeldahl, Peter. "Warhol in Bloom." *The New Yorker* 11 Mar. 2002: 82–84.

Updike, John. "Fast Art: The Sweatless Creations of Andy Warhol." *The New Republic* 27 Mar. 1989: 26–28.

Resources

Selected Bibliography

Bourdon, David. *Warhol*. New York: Henry N. Abrams, 1989.

Colacello, Bob. *Holy Terror: Andy Warhol Close Up*. New York: HarperCollins, 1990.

Koestenbaum, Wayne. *Andy Warhol*. New York: Lipper/ Viking Books, 2001.

Scherman, Tony, and David Dalton. *Pop: The Genius of Andy Warhol*. New York: HarperCollins, 2009.

The Staff of The Andy Warhol Museum. *Andy Warhol: 365 Takes*. New York: Harry N. Abrams, 2004.

Further Reading

Aronson, Marc. *Art Attack: A Brief Cultural History of the Avant-Garde*. New York: Clarion, 1998.

Bolton, Linda. *Andy Warhol*. New York: Franklin Watts, 2002.

Greenberg, Jan, and Sandra Jordon. *Andy Warhol: Prince of Pop*. New York: Delacorte, 2004.

Yoe, Craig, and Janet Morra-yoe. *The Art of Mickey Mouse*. New York: Hyperion, 1991.

Web Links

To learn more about critiquing the works of Andy Warhol, visit ABDO Publishing Company online at **www.abdopublishing.com**. Web sites about the works of Andy Warhol are featured on our Book Links page. These links are routinely monitored and updated to provide the most current information available.

For More Information

The Andy Warhol Museum

117 Sandusky Street, Pittsburgh, PA 15212

412-237-8300

www.warhol.org

The Andy Warhol Museum features art and archival resources related to Andy Warhol.

The Museum of Modern Art

11 West 53 Street, New York, NY 10019

212-708-9400

www.moma.org

The Museum of Modern Art features extensive collections of modern art, including works by Andy Warhol and other Pop artists.

Source Notes

Chapter 1. Introduction to Critiques
None.

Chapter 2. A Closer Look at Andy Warhol
1. Bob Colacello. *Holy Terror: Andy Warhol Close Up*. New York: HarperCollins, 1990. 25.
2. The Andy Warhol Foundation for the Visual Arts. *Mission and Overview*. 4 Jan. 2010 <http://www.warholfoundation.org/foundation/overview.html>.

Chapter 3. An Overview of *32 Campbell's Soup Cans*
None.

Chapter 4. How to Apply Reception Theory to *32 Campbell's Soup Cans*
1. Robert Hughes. *American Visions: The Epic History of Art in America*. New York: Alfred A. Knopf, 1997. 540.
2. Steven Henry Madoff, ed. *Pop Art: A Critical History*. Berkeley: University of California Press, 1997. 267.

Chapter 5. An Overview of *Turquoise Marilyn* and *16 Jackies*

None.

Chapter 6. How to Apply Biographical Criticism to *Turquoise Marilyn* and *16 Jackies*

1. Andy Warhol. *The Philosophy of Andy Warhol (From A to B and Back Again)*. New York: Harcourt, Brace & Inc., 1975. 49.

2. Tony Scherman and David Dalton. *Pop: The Genius of Andy Warhol*. New York: HarperCollins, 2009. 217.

3. Pam Meecham and Julie Sheldon. *Modern Art: A Critical Introduction*. 2nd ed. New York: Routledge, 2005. 242.

Chapter 7. An Overview of *Brillo Boxes*

1. The Staff of The Andy Warhol Museum. *Andy Warhol: 365 Takes*. New York: Harry N. Abrams, 2004. 35.

Source Notes Continued

Chapter 8. How to Apply Marxist Theory to *Brillo Boxes*

1. Steven Henry Madoff, ed. *Pop Art: A Critical History*. Berkeley: University of California Press, 1997. 275.

2. Tony Scherman and David Dalton. *Pop: The Genius of Andy Warhol*. New York: HarperCollins, 2009. 51.

3. Ibid. 79.

Chapter 9. An Overview of *Mickey Mouse*

None.

Chapter 10. How to Apply Formalist Criticism to *Mickey Mouse*

1. Pam Meecham and Julie Sheldon. *Modern Art: A Critical Introduction*. 2nd ed. New York: Routledge, 2005. 26.

Index

Index Continued

About the Author

Michael Fallon is an artist, arts writer, and nonprofit administrator based in Saint Paul, Minnesota. Fallon received a Master in Fine Arts in book arts from the University of Alabama. As a book artist, he worked with legendary figures such as Kurt Vonnegut, John Barth, Nikki Giovanni, and Robert Bly. Since 1998, Fallon has written reviews, feature articles, essays, and profiles on art for various publications. Today, Fallon is working on various writing projects and doing nonprofit work for institutions of higher education.

Photo Credits